GOD GOALS

Connecting With God During The Crisis And
Chaos

Shanté D. Berry

GOD GOALS

Berry Best Books
Publishing Co.

Copyright © 2021 by Berry Best Books Publishing Co.

Book design & editing by Shanté D. Berry : Cherie Banks

February 2021, First Edition

ISBN 978-0-578-84834-1

An Imprint of Berry Best Books Publishing
www.shanteberry.com@berrybestpublish

Ordering Information:

Available through Amazon, Barnes and Noble, and Kindle.

Special discounts are available on quantity purchases by

corporations, associations, educators, and others.

For details, contact the publisher at the above listed address.

For my family and friends, Hope City church in Houston, Texas & Millennials on the Move!

Thank you for loving me, encouraging me, and seeing me and who I am in Christ Jesus! I love you!

Thank you to all of my day one supporters, friends and family and future readers for your support, patience and positivity help tremendously in achieving my God Goals!

Contents

Foreward

"Set your minds on things above, not on earthly things. For you died, and your life is now hidden with Christ in God. When Christ, who is your life, appears, then you also will appear with him in glory." (Colossians 3:2-4)

M y name is Chris Destin and I am minister out of Christ Holy Temple Deliverance Church in Houston, Texas where I serve under Bishop Jimmy Singleton. I had the privilege of meeting Ms. Shanté Berry not long ago but it was undeniably obvious that she was different. She was not only beautiful externally but radiant internally and has a clear understanding of the call God has on her life. She knows that only the things we do for Christ will last so while it may be good to you, if it's not in God's plan then it won't be good for you.

Shanté understands that instinctively we all desire to seek out the validation or approval of others through ratings, sales, likes, comparisons, and applauses. We are in a constant scramble seeking out good money, good wives, good husbands, good schools, good neighborhoods, good churches, and ultimately the things that society declares good. We may do this to validate who we are through what we have externally vs who we are internally. Now don't get me wrong, these things are not bad things and it is absolutely nothing wrong with desiring a good healthy life because God wants you to also have a good life!

In (John 10:10) Christ said he came that we might have life and life more abundantly but the question is like he asked the rich young ruler in (Matthew 19:16-30) "What is Good?" He told the young ruler only God is good and the eternal life you desire is through following his commandments. The rich young ruler thought he was good to go for he told Christ that he had kept the commandments all his life but doing good works and being a good work of God is not the same. God looks at the heart or intent of a man and not his external acts. So Jesus asked him if he wanted to be perfect to sell everything he had, give to the poor, and follow Christ. For his treasure would be in heaven and not on earth but the young ruler could not because he was rich and his mind was still bound to the validation of his possessions. So the external approval of man was more important to the ruler than obtaining eternal life! He just desired to do good in hopes he could continue to be rewarded here on earth. To do a good work in Christ and be apart of God's plan to restore the Kingdom was too great of a price to pay.

The Bible declares in (Matthew 6:33) to seek ye first the kingdom of God and ALL his righteousness, and all these things will be added unto you. Seeking God's plan in your life is where you find perfect peace to sustain yourself through life because you understand that everything outside of his plan is temporary. Only the things you do for God will last and give you the peace you need to surpass the understanding of man. God's plan can only be discerned through the Holy Spirit and this spirit is only given to those who obey him.

In God's plan, you are free to the bondage of approval by man nor waiting on society to justify you through culture because who God has called he has justified, and who God has justified he has also glorified. (Romans 8:30) For who Christ has set free is free indeed! (John 8:36) Set yourself free from the common sense of man and know that we now have the mind of Christ where there is no condemnation! Common sense condemns all that is not common to culture but Christ did not die for us to be common but for us to be Holy! Set apart in Love for the purpose of our Father who loves us unconditionally. So if we are not careful we will allow common sense to abort God's Plan in our life through the frustration of trying to fit eternal life in a temporary world.

3

So in closing the purpose of this devotional guide is to highlight the importance of discerning your good ideas from God's plan in your life and aid you in growing closer to God throughout the storms of life. Ms. Berry emphasizes that you must know that what's good to man is only what can benefit the plan of man but God's plan is that which will benefit His kingdom. "But you are a chosen people, a royal priesthood, a holy nation, God's special possession, that you may declare the praises of him who called you out of darkness into his wonderful light." (1 Peter 2:9)

Chris Destin, Minister

Houston, Texas

Introduction

The era that we are currently in has not been easy on ANY of us! It's been quite crazy in fact. From the constant negativity in the news, police brutality and aggression, racial tension, civil arrest, protest, sickness, disease, despair, loss of life...it's A LOT! It is enough to make your head spin. Even as Christians, we walk and talk the word of God, but we can get overwhelmed and burnt out sometimes. Burnt out of zoom call, burnt out on work, family, and friends. One thing we can't get burnt out on is God. If you are a Christian you picked up the right book! If you are not a Christian, you picked up the right book! What better time in the life to turn your life over to Christ. Even in the darkness he sees you and wants you to draw close to him. It is not by accident that you were drawn to this book, turn to page 104 for a special prayer just for you. In my spirit, I know that through all this pain, suffering, and turmoil something amazing is going to emerge in the Kingdom of God. The bible says do not conform to the pattern of this world but be transformed by the renewing of your mind. (Romans 12:2) The year 2020 was marked by multiple crises, and we remain hopeful that 2021 and beyond will bring the end of this terrible pandemic and the struggle and inequity it exacerbated. I want to take a moment to thank you for purchasing a copy of this guide & devotional and keeping the faith. You are planting a seed in not only my book ministry but staying dedicated to your own and growth and further the Kingdom of God.

Good without God simply isn't enough. Vision without God is in vain. Your vision needs to come from God so that you can do it to give glory to God. Where there is no vision the people perish. (Proverbs 29:18) The beginning of a new season is the perfect time to reset our minds, look closely at our habits, and prepare our hearts for what God is going to do next. There is a big difference in having good goals set for the year, but what about having God goals set? So often do we hear about relationship goals, financial goals, boss goals, and whatever category you can think of? A good idea is NOT necessarily a God idea. It's time to not only anticipate our own personal goals in life but also God's goals and take time out to focus on how he can propel us closer to our purpose in life. It's time to move forward!

Let us start with some of the critical keys to moving forward and setting the atmosphere for connecting with God and setting God Goals :

Carve out time with God every day.

You will seek me and find me when you seek me with all your heart. (Jeremiah 29:13) Start rebuilding healthy God goals by making time with God as your top priority. When you prioritize time with Him, you allow Him to renew your mind and change the way you think. It is thirty minutes a day make the time. Be creative in your connection.

Start your day with a bible story or devotional plan and get into the habit of letting God's Word speak to you. Set up your day with praise and purpose by putting on praise and worship music in the morning as you start your day.

Ask yourself: At what times of day do I find it easiest and hardest to connect with God? Morning, Noon, or night?

Remember whose you are

You are not your own, for you were bought with a price. So glorify God in your body. (1 Corinthians 6:19-20) Everything you've sacrificed this past year will never compare to the ultimate sacrifice God made for you. When you begin to grow discouraged, remember that God is eternally invested in your life. Your future is in the hands of someone who loves you and adores you. God wants you to become the person He created you to be. Glorifying God in your body requires that you be mindful of what you eat, drink, absorb through media, and entertainment as well. Your body is your temple in which you can't move out. Set up your day by being intentional about honoring your temple.

Ask yourself: What goals will help me glorify God more?

Start small goals first

One who is faithful in a very little is also faithful in much, and one who is dishonest in a very little is also dishonest in much. (Luke 16:10) All it takes is the first step to start moving towards a new direction. Growth and transformation take time, just pick something small you'd like to change, and start there. Consistently doing one thing well will make it easier to master other habits and goals later. And if you miss a day, give yourself grace. Starting small makes it easier to pick yourself back up and keep moving forward in the right direction.

Ask yourself: What is one thing I can start to master executing small goals first?

Invite others to join you on this journey

As iron sharpens iron, so one person sharpens another. (Proverbs 27:17) We were not meant to go through life alone, for the bible says it is not good for man to be alone. You'll find it easier to stay on track if you invite some friends to join you on your journey. Try joining a connect group (Millennials on the Move!) or downloading the bible app and then commit to working through a plan together.

Ask yourself: What trusted friends can I invite to join me?

As you keep developing healthy habits, over time you will find yourself becoming more like the person God created you to be.

It only takes a minute to get going, and these critical steps are a great place to begin. Select what area you want to focus on first, and then stay committed to moving forward.

CHAPTER 1

Good Goals Vs God Goals

"In their hearts humans plan their course, but the Lord establishes their steps." (Proverbs 16:9)

The goals we set for ourselves can be great and amazing. But do they involve God and the will He has for our life? Good without God simply isn't enough. We always want more. More money, more blessings, more territory, more friends, but do we want more of God? The goals, scriptures, action items, and prayers outlined throughout this book will help you shift your focus to desiring more of the God Goals and less of the good goals.

They will also help you have better discernment on what is good and what is God and operate in the Holy Spirit and less in you flesh. If you starve your flesh your spirit will grow. If you feed you flesh you will ultimately exist and operate in the carnality of that We have to be intentional about our plans to make God-ordained and destined decisions. Our decisions shape our every way of life.

A goal without consistency is a wish. Thoughts become things when we are consistent and working towards them. Make i happen! I am a planner. I have written and planned so many things out in my life. At one point in time, I had each year of my life planned up to age 25. As a teenager, I thought it all would come true. When it didn't I ask God, "Well why not?!" Turns out He had other plans. Better plans at that. Can you ever look back in your life and rejoice that God didn't give you the goals and desires you wanted? I sure can. What I thought I needed was simply a want and a lot of my desires were carnal and temporary. I was praying for a snack while God wanted to give me soul food. What goals have you not been able to accomplish for years and years? That is not an indication to give up, however, it is an invitation to invite God in to review your goals. When you silence your fears and trust God, and His timing it is incredible what you can accomplish. You must be willing to nurture, develop, and transition your goals into God goals.

Ask yourself: What goals will help me intensify my goals to focus them on God more?

_____

_____

_____

_____

_____

_____

_____

_____

_____

_____

_____

_____

_____

_____

_____

_____

_____

_____

_____

_____

_____

_____

_____

_____

_____

_____

_____

_____

_____

_____

_____

_____

_____

_____

_____

God Goals

☐ Make a list of all of your goals this year, this month, this week, and bring them before God and ask for clarity about what that goal is just good and which God centered goal.

☐ Read your bible. Everyday. It may sound cliché, however the more you fill up with the word of God, the more your spirit will fill in the gaps. There are several ways to read the bible. Hard copy, audio, or e-book, let's find a way.

☐ Implement worship everyday. In your own way, find time to worship every day. This can be through music, meditation, singing, walking, or even while you're working out.

☐ Once you receive confirmation on your God goals, go to God in prayer about timing. Some God goals will not be accomplished overnight or even in this year. Be patient with the process.

Scripture Meditations

The plans of the LORD stand firm forever, the purposes of His heart through all generations. (Psalm 33:11)

For the LORD Almighty has planned, and who can thwart Him? His hand is stretched out, and who can turn it back? (Isaiah 14:27)

No longer will there be any curse. The throne of God and of the Lam will be in the city, and His servants will serve Him. They will see His face, and His name will be on their foreheads. There will be no night. They will not need the light of a lamp or the light of the sun, for the Lord God will give them life. And they will reign forever and ever. (Revelations 22)

There is a way *that seems* right to a man, but its end *is* the way of death. (Proverbs 14:12)

Now to him who is able to do immeasurably more than all we ask or imagine, according to His power that is at work within us, to him be glory in the church and in Christ Jesus throughout all generations, for ever and ever! Amen. (Ephesians 3:20-21)

For I know the plans I have for you, declares the LORD, plans to prosper you and not to harm you, plans to give you hope and a future. (Jerimiah 29:11)

Be not transformed by the world but renew your mind.

(Roman 12:2)

Prayer

Heavenly Fatherly, I thank you for this day. I pray that when I am making plans and decisions help me submit myself and my plans to you. Speak to my heart Lord and direct all of my steps. I pray that you continue to grow and mature me. Help me to love the pursuit of wisdom, growth, and keep you at the center of my life and continue to pursue oneness with you. Help me to listen intently and mold me into a new man/woman of understanding.

Amen

CHAPTER 2

Jesus Take The Wheel

And he said to all, "If anyone would come after me, let him deny himself and take up His cross daily and follow me. (Luke 9:23)

G iving God the control is easier said than done. But what we should realize is that God is all-knowing and all-powerful so God is in control already. Why you are trying to figure it out, guess what?! God has already worked it out! Surrendering to God is as simple as us laying our will and desires down at the feet of Jesus and allowing God to do His will. As humans, naturally we want to know what's next, we want a preview of the coming attractions. That's not always possible. Your steps are already ordered. Surrendering your will to God. Your soul is your mind, will, and emotions. When you surrender your thoughts, emotions, and will to God your energy is directed to him and not the world. Cry out to God for your needs and he will give you peace, redirection, and answers. Making up your mind that you do not have to operate in your flesh every day yet operate in the Holy Spirit.

I remember a time when I literally had to allow Jesus to take the wheel. I was living in Phoenix, AZ as a full-fledged young career woman in the banking industry. On my way to work one day, I was stopped at a red light and a Ford F-150 pickup truck trampled into the back of my car. My glasses flew off my face, and the In-N-Out burger in my hand slammed into the front windshield. As my body jerked rapidly, my head also hit the window. What just happened?

I was only a block away from my destination when my car was hit, sliding me into the next lane. I quickly regained control of my car and pulled over to the side of the street. I was impressed with how rapid my reflexes were and somehow the car avoided hitting any other cars. Then I fell into complete shock from what just happened. Because of the trauma, I didn't experience any pain. However, when I tried to get out of the car, my whole body became instantly stiff. Since I was hurt, I sat in my car and called the police.

Still in shock, I pushed my way straight to the hospital. A few x-rays were taken, and I was released to go home. I contemplated taking the rest of the week off work because my body was unstable and ached. I didn't want to let my team down, so I pulled it together and went to work. My car was completely totaled. I was devastated but I realized it could have been much worse. God was in complete control. I went through six months of physical therapy but God gave me complete peace about the situation. I had to surrender everything to God, although I was by myself in Arizona, I knew I was not alone. Jesus took the wheel. Likewise, when we surrender ourselves and our will to God, we choose what He wants instead of what we want, we demonstrate our love of God.

Ask yourself: What goals will help me surrender to God more?

_____

_____

_____

_____

_____

_____

_____

_____

_____

_____

_____

_____

_____

_____

God Goals

☐ Read your bible. Everyday. It sounds cliché, however the more you fill up with the word of God, the more your spirit will fill in the gaps. There are several ways to read the bible. Hard copy, audio, or e-book, let's find a way.

☐ Implement worship everyday. In your own way, find time to worship every day. This can be through music, meditation, singing, walking, or even while you're working out.

☐ Once you receive confirmation on your God goals, go to God in prayer about timing. Some God goals will not be accomplished overnight or even in this year. Be patient with the process.

☐ Surrender your desires and wants to God first. Oftentimes we want what we want and we go to God with our mind made up. Practice going to God first for your answers rather than making up your own mind.

Scripture Meditations

Submit yourselves therefore to God. Resist the devil, and he will flee from you. (James 4:7)

Finally, be strong in the Lord and in the strength of His might. Put on the whole armor of God, that you may be able to stand against the schemes of the devil. For we do not wrestle against flesh and blood, but against the rulers, against the authorities, against the cosmic powers over this present darkness, against the spiritual forces of evil in the heavenly places (Ephesians 6:10-12)

Humble yourselves before the Lord, and he will exalt you. (James 4:10)

My son, give me your heart, and let your eyes observe my ways (Proverbs 23:26)

But be doers of the word, and not hearers only, deceiving yourselves. (James 1:22)

Draw near to God, and he will draw near to you. Cleanse your hands, you sinners, and purify your hearts, you double-minded (James 4:8)

Prayer

Heavenly Father, help me let go of pride, control, and the desire to be right in my own eyes. Humble me oh Lord as I accept that my steps are already ordered and ordained by you Lord. Guide me each day as I move around and carry your glory. I pray that I will not be conceited or seek self-gain. If there is any selfishness in my heart please remove it Lord. Help me put others needs above my own, serve, help and see others and also assert healthy boundaries were they should be. May pride and control never get in the way of me doing what is right. I pray that I am never afraid to ask for help or prayer or show emotion. Help me to be meek, gentle, and kind yet brave, assertive, and bold in my faith. Help me know and understand my significance and value and just how much you love me.

In Jesus name I pray, Amen

CHAPTER 3

Jesus Help Me Heal

"Then your light shall break forth like the morning, Your healing shall spring forth speedily, And your righteousness shall go before you; The glory of the LORD shall be your rear guard." (Isaiah 58:8)

There is a lot going on in the times that we live in. In our world, homes, houses, and minds. As a millennial I have experienced several historic and tragic events. By the grace of God, I've lived through hurricanes, pandemics, civil unrest riots, and economic crisis. I feel like I have seen it all. One might ask, what's next? The most certain thing I know that it is all in God's hands and everything has purpose for situations don't just happen to us but it is happening for us. Healing mind, body, and spirit takes time but it also takes recognition and willingness on your part to do the work. We are human. Tragic experiences at times can produce trauma. We cannot go through life triggered at every corner of life. It's time to heal.

Accepting where you are is a critical component of healing from a traumatic storm in your life. Where there is a tragedy, there is a loss. Where there is a loss, there is grief. The stages of grief range from denial, anger, depression, and acceptance. I had a significant transformation when I connected with positive and healing sources. This made a considerable difference for me during my storm.

You can exercise turning your pain into progress. Keeping your mindset healthy and focused during the storm is necessary for healing and development. Embracing the spirit of depression will cause you to be defeated. Some of the most painful times in your life can also be the most progressive. You can use negative energy to push the positive out. Exhale the fear, doubt, depression, and negativity. Inhale fearlessness, gratitude, confidence, and happiness. The sooner you apply this, the quicker you can create room for opportunities to appear. Creating short term goals are an essential part of growth because it gives you attainable and measurable benchmarks that you can achieve every day.

When a traumatic situation happen in life this can create trauma that can remain in our lives if we don't heal. Situational trauma also can involve triggers the effect how you respond emotionally to different situations. Our emotions can be tied to an event, person, or place where the trauma happened and those memories can create anxiety, depression, lack of self-esteem, fear, and doubt. It is important to seek professional help when you have those symptoms. Talking through your trauma and healing is a process. It is something that can stay with us and the pain can spill over into every aspect of our lives if we do not heal properly. Do not be ashamed of taking care of your mental health. While your wounds in life are probably not your fault, your healing is your responsibility.

If you're continually cutting people out of your life instead of building relationships and connections that enhance your life, it is time for you to heal and address the source of the pain and anger. While I believe some people are in your life for a season, if you make burning bridges a habit you will eventually start forest fires. It is time to put the forest fires out of your life. You can't get to your purpose if you refuse to look back into your past and heal from situations that hurt you.

If you don't heal, your life will reveal recycled anger, fear, doubt, and sadness. Find a safe space with a confidant or counselor to help you process your difficult life experiences. You cannot heal what you refuse to deal with. Everybody may have an old scar, but if you continue to put a band-aid over a bullet wound, you will not heal properly.

Ask yourself: What goals will help me heal from my pain & glorif
God?

_____

_____

_____

_____

_____

_____

_____

_____

_____

_____

_____

_____

_____

_____

_____

_____

_____

_____

_____

_____

_____

_____

_____

_____

_____

_____

_____

_____

_____

God Goals

☐ Schedule time to talk with a mental health professional. Everyone needs counseling in some form, we are human. A counselor can assist you in your healing and can really change the trajectory of your life. (www.betterhelp.com or www.faithfulcounseling.com) The options are easy and affordable.

☐ Make of list of anything that you feel weighs you down this could be triggers, unforgiveness, anger, sadness, or rage. Ask God to search your heart and reveal those things. "Search me, God, and know my heart; test me and know my anxious thoughts. See if there is any offensive way in me, and lead me in the way everlasting." (Psalm 139:23-24)

☐ List out who your confidants are. Who can you confide in and ask for prayer? If you don't have any confidants pray and ask God to send the right people into your life who you can trust and confide in when your heart is heavy.

☐ Schedule 10-15 minutes of prayer and/or meditation daily. Meditate on the word of God. Empty you mind from the noises that can consume our minds throughout the day.

Practice mindfulness.

☐ Establish firm boundaries that are dedicated to your healing. Enforce them with confidence. If your boundary with yourself is no social media for a week, or no texting while your at work, set it and stick to it.

Scripture Meditations

Praise the LORD, my soul, and forget not all His benefits who forgives all your sins and heals all your diseases, who redeems your life from the pit and crowns you with love and compassion. (Psalm 103: 2-4)

Dear friend, I pray that you may enjoy good health and that all may go well with you, even as your soul is getting along well (3 John: 2)

He himself bore our sins" in His body on the cross, so that we might die to sins and live for righteousness; "by His wounds you have been healed. (1 Peter 2:24)

In my name they will drive out demons; they will speak in new tongues; they will pick up snakes with their hands; and when they drink deadly poison, it will not hurt them at all; they will place their hands on sick people, and they will get well. (Mark 16:17 -18)

Jesus called His twelve disciples to him and gave them authority to drive out impure spirits and to heal every disease and sickness. (Matthew 10:1)

A wicked messenger falls into trouble, but a trustworthy envoy brings healing. (Proverbs 13:17)

Gracious words are a honeycomb, sweet to the soul and healing to the bones. (Proverbs 16:24)

Prayer

Heavenly Father, I thank you for creating me. Thank you for giving me a soul filled with your Holy Spirit. I pray right now that I can surrender my pain, trauma, and any past hurt to you Jesus. Make my heart whole. Soften my heart and help my find ways to yield to you in humbleness. I pray for protection and discernment. Please remove any temptation of evil that is attempting to make me fall. Lord I ask for more of what you have to give. Help me experience the power of your life at work in me, and your beautiful life flowing through me. Replenish what's been stolen or lost. Fill me to overflowing with what comes from you. When I feel troubled and unable to do simple things, I choose to receive new strength. You are fully alive and you renew my life. When I feel shaken, you are not. You never cease to offer love and compassion for those who are weary. When I can't figure out what to do next and it feels like everything I do is wrong, your arms remain open to receive me. I can't understand your acceptance and love, but you offer it. Help me accept it. Help me reach out to others when I need help, encouragement as well. Give me courage to ask for what I need and the courage to offer the same for others. Heal my heart and mind in all the areas that keep me closed off, isolated, withdrawn, or defensive in relationships. When my mind spirals and my thoughts are filled with negative things, nudge me towards you and what you have for me instead. Strengthen my mind and open my heart Lord.

In Jesus name I pray, Amen

CHAPTER 4

Peace Be Still

You will keep in perfect peace those whose minds are steadfast because they trust in you. (Isaiah 26:3)

The chaotic, crazy, and unstable times are vital. They challenge you to rise to a high level of consciousness and help you to become a problem-solver. You are more alert and aware of the situations around you. Peace isn't the absence of trouble. Rather it is the response and reflection of us trusting God despite the trouble. You can be knee-deep in the midst of great trials and troubled waters but have a peaceful presence. We should constantly be anchored in the Lord. This allows your faith to become stronger by talking and walking with God a lot more. What would happen if you did this every day? What if you let God speak to you or you spent more time with Him? Imagine being receptive to the voice of God through your everyday experiences. Carve out a special place and time to spend with God. As a child of God, I dwell in His presence and wait for His direction. As a Bride of God, I want His face to shine upon me and be pleased with the life that I'm living.

Peace starts within and it radiates outside. It shows up in everything that you do. Ushering in peace into your life requires you to be okay with solitude. Learn to be okay with being alone. Adjust to being okay in the stillness of quietness in your house. Don't allow the business of each day to clutter out the voice of God. There are a lot of voices that we can hear throughout the day. Our own voice, friends, family, & the opinions, attitudes, and beliefs that we read from social media. Fasting and praying are so important as we navigate through life. Alone does not mean lonely. Utilize your alone time as a time of gratitude. If you are single, you can be happily single. If you are always continually dating or talking to someone, it can serve as a distraction to the work that God is doing in your life. Sometimes God needs to isolate you before He can elevate you. If you are married, this is a perfect opportunity to share intimacy through prayer and strengthening your connection with your spouse. Create times to pray and fast together. It's those quiet times at night or early in the morning when you can hear God's voice speak to you. He just needs you to be still. Don't drown him out with noise and people who don't honor you or erve a higher purpose in your life.

Ask yourself: What goals will help me usher in peace & glorify God more?

_____

_____

_____

_____

_____

_____

_____

_____

_____

_____

_____

_____

_____

_____

_____

_____

_____

_____

_____

_____

_____

_____

_____

_____

_____

_____

_____

_____

_____

_____

_____

_____

_____

_____

_____

God Goals

☐ Create a space in your house that will serve as a prayer area, anoint it and keep it clean and open. This could be a closet, spare bedroom , or even your car.

☐ Peace is a gift from God and we must learn to defend it relentlessly. **God is the source of peace.** Make God your rock- **He is stronger than all of your circumstances.**

☐ The Bible tells us, "Put on the full armor of God, that you may be able to stand against the schemes of the Devil" (Ephesians 6:11). There are so many lies that we will encounter on a daily basis that will try and steal our peace. Ask the Spirit of God to bring you greater awareness of those lies that are not only infiltrating, but also devastating your life. Declare your need for His strength and power to expel the lies that steal from the peace-filled life you are given through Christ.

☐ We are right in the middle of a great battle, with the Devil attacking your thoughts and challenging our emotions. We have to focus on what God is Doing and wants to do in your life.

Scripture Meditations

"'I will grant peace in the land, and you will lie down and no one will make you afraid. I will remove wild beasts from the land, and the sword will not pass through your country. (Leviticus 26:6)

The LORD turns His face toward you and give you peace. (Numbers 6:26)

Her ways are ways of pleasantness, and all her paths are peace. (Proverbs 3:2)

You will keep in perfect peace those whose minds are steadfast, because they trust in you. (Isaiah 26:3)

The LORD gives strength to His people; the LORD blesses His people with peace. (Psalm 29:11)

Peace I leave with you; my peace I give you. I do not give to you as the world gives. Do not let your hearts be troubled and do not be afraid. (John 14:27)

Great peace has those who love your law, and nothing can make them stumble. (Psalm 119:165)

Let the peace of Christ rule in your hearts, since

As members of one body you were called to peace. And be thankful. (Colossians 3:15)

Finally, brothers and sisters, rejoice! Strive for full restoration, encourage one another, be of one mind, live in peace. And the God of love and peace will be with you. (2 Corinthians 13:11)

Prayer

Heavenly Father, I pray to experience an abundant peace and calmness in my life. If there is anything in my life that is causing me to be anxious, fearful, or worried, I pray that I can stop and surrender those thoughts to you and present my worries and requests to You. I pray anxious thoughts never consume my mind and may your peace guard me always. Overwhelm my soul and spirit with the security of your presence. When a storm arises, may your peace comfort me. When things do not add up or make any sense to me, continue to calm my spirit. When I am confused Lord, let your peace help me discern the truth. When conflict arises may your peace bring resolution. I pray that you allow me to understand how thankfulness can combat worry. Extinguish any fears and anxious thoughts right now in Jesus name. Fill me with your peace so I can live confidently in you Jesus! You are the only enduring source of peace in a world full of anger and frustration. I do not know what will happen in the future, my life is filled with highs and lows that I do not understand. Help me not to sin in my anger. May I have faith in your peace that will never fail. May your word refresh my spirit, renew my soul and empower me to live like you Prince of Peace, thank you that you hear and answer my prayers. Today I ask you to bless me with perfect peace. Remove annoyance and animosity from my life and replace them with steadfast trust in you. Fill my heart with compassion instead of conflict, humility instead of hatred and faith instead of fury. Be exalted above the heavens. Let your glory be above all the earth.

In Jesus name I pray, Amen

CHAPTER 05

Trusting God

"The young lions lack and suffer hunger; But those who seek the LORD shall not lack any good thing" (Psalm 34:10)

Trust isn't a thought or feeling. It's an act and practice that you walk out in your daily life. It's a muscle that needs to be exercised. If you've never used this muscle, it's going to be weak and wobbly at first. When I get back in the gym after a short break I have to stretch. Stretch those trust muscles and remember who is in charge. If I quickly take off running, lactic acid can build up quickly, I may quickly catch my legs cramping!

Knowing who you are is reassuring in the tests, trials, and setbacks that are a definitive part of life. God has equipped you with everything you need to survive. He enables you to bear up under your burdens by His grace. Never forget that God has handpicked your circumstances to accomplish a specific purpose. Your life has no finish line. The progress, blessings, and miracles are on the other side of your doubt, fear, stagnancy. Your vision board or planner may seem stagnant right now, but when we trust that His plans are better than our own, we are fully trusting and believing in God's plans.

Ask yourself: What goals will help me trust God more?

_____

_____

_____

_____

_____

_____

_____

_____

_____

_____

_____

_____

_____

_____

_____

_____

_____

_____

_____

_____

_____

_____

_____

_____

_____

_____

_____

_____

_____

_____

_____

_____

_____

_____

_____

_____

_____

God Goals

- ☐ Make a list the problems that you have faced and how God came through on those problems. Constantly remind yourself of His miraculous provision.

- ☐ Tithe! Tithing is not a head issue it is a trust issue, Trust God by giving Him the first fruit and allow /Him to

- ☐ Don't compare your life to other or allow others to try to compare. Comparison is the thief of joy and God has a uniquely designed path just for you.

- ☐ Pray without Ceasing. God is listening to you.

- ☐ Don't let a dark season determine your destiny. Praise him in the darkness, for he is developing you in the darkness.

- ☐ Be Still. Remember that God knows the bigger picture.

- ☐ Crawl, walk, jog, then Run! Today take one step towards Jesus

Scripture Meditations

A man's steps are of the Lord; how then can a man understand His own way. (Proverbs 20:24)

For God did not give us a spirit of fear, but of spirit of power, of love, and of a sound mind. (2 Timothy 2:15)

Surely God is my salvation; I will trust and not be afraid. The LORD, the LORD himself, is my strength and my defense; he has become my salvation." (Isaiah 12:2)

You will keep in perfect peace those whose minds are steadfast, because they trust in you. (Isaiah 26:3)

Do not let your hearts be troubled. You believe in God; believe also in me. (John 14:1)

Trust in the LORD forever, for the LORD, the LORD himself, is the Rock eternal. (Isaiah 26:4)

Have I not commanded you? Be strong and courageous. Do not be afraid; do not be discouraged, for the LORD your God will be with you wherever you go." (Joshua 1:9)

Some trust in chariots and some in horses, but we trust in the name of the LORD our God. (**Psalm 20:7**)

Ask yourself: What goals will help me Trust God more?

The LORD is my strength and my shield; my heart trusts in him, and he helps me. My heart leaps for joy, and with my song I praise him. Psalm 28:7

Many are the woes of the wicked, but the LORD's unfailing love surrounds the one who trusts in him. Psalm 32:10

Prayer

Lord, I thank You that You are the God of the impossible. You can do anything. I want to trust in Your ability and not my own. Teach me to see difficulties in my life from Your perspective. Help me to focus on You and Your power. I want to be like Joshua and Caleb who believed in a good report and focused on You even in hard circumstances (Numbers 14:7-9). My responsibility is to carefully read, trust, and obey Your Word. Today I bring before You this difficulty in my life (Name a hard situation you are right now facing). Help me not to fear but to trust You in this situation. I declare my faith in Your ability to fulfill Your promises to me. You will fight for me and win the battles in my life. You are mighty, powerful, righteous, and true. Lord, please forgive me for my lack of faith. So often I cry out in fear, I know I will always need you, but please help me to rely on you more! I pray I can trust you in the area of my life, my relationships, my career, my finances. May your power sustain me and may I live in the confidence of your provision for me. You are a loving God and I appreciate your love, grace, patience, mercy, and your might! Thank you for everything you do. May your will be done in my life as I TRUST in you!

In Jesus name I pray, Amen

CHAPTER 06

Loving God

"To know the love of Christ which passes knowledge; that you may be filled with all the fullness of God. (Ephesians 3:19)

L oving God more doesn't just happen all by itself. If we want to love God with all our heart, mind, soul and strength, then we have to do our part to staying connected to God. We have to constantly feed and strengthen our spirit by studying the Bible, talking to God regularly, freely forgiving others, denying our self and our way, and rejecting worldliness. should not be optional, it should be a priority. Even Jesus himself needed His alone time with the Father. What makes us that that we don't need that as well?

Ask yourself: What goals will help me Love God more?

_____

_____

_____

_____

_____

_____

_____

_____

_____

_____

_____

_____

_____

_____

_____

_____

_____

_____

_____

_____

_____

_____

_____

_____

_____

_____

_____

_____

_____

_____

_____

_____

_____

_____

God Goals

☐ Examine your own heart to see what ways you are being too selfish and wrapped in yourself. Give those areas to the Lord, and seek His will for your life.

☐ Make your time with God a priority, not an option

☐ Increase your obedience in God's word. Let's not just be hearers of the word but doers of the word as well.

☐ Make prayer a must. Lack of prayer is a sign of unbelief and pride. Practice having daily conversations with God, morning, noon, and night.

☐ Practice Forgiveness daily. If are heart is so heavy with unforgiveness, how we operate in and receive God's love?" But if you do not forgive men their trespasses, neither will your Father forgive your trespasses" (Matthew 6:15).

Scripture Meditations

"If you love me, keep my commands. (John 14:15)

Love the LORD your God with all your heart and with all your soul and with all your strength. (Deuteronomy 6:5)

Love the LORD your God and keep His requirements, His decrees His laws and His commands always. (Deuteronomy 11:1)

So if you faithfully obey the commands I am giving you today— to love the LORD your God and to serve him with all your heart and with all your soul (Deuteronomy 11:13)

and that you may love the LORD your God, listen to His voice, and hold fast to him. For the LORD is your life, and he will give you many years in the land he swore to give to your fathers, Abraham, Isaac and Jacob. (Deuteronomy 30:20)

Love is patient and kind; love does not envy or boast; it is not arrogant or rude. It does not insist on its own way; it is not irritable or resentful; it does not rejoice at wrongdoing but rejoices with the truth. Love bears all things, believes all things, hopes all things, endures all things. Love never ends. (1 Corinthians 13:4-8)

Prayer

Heavenly Father I thank you for being a wonderful, beautiful, and shining example of love. Thank You for loving me. I am forever amazed by the power of love and how it can transform lives. My prayer is that I continue to pursue an intimate relationship with you Jesus. Help me to know real love because I know you. Holy Spirit fill my heart with your presence and help me to love like Christ. Motivate me daily by Your love to love all people. Inspire me to go the extra mile to be a blessing to those around us, and those less fortunate. I pray that I will take advantage of every day I am given to spend time in your presence. Allow the passion of my heart continues to keep me serving you. Help me be determined to keep your commandments. I pray that I can be a man/woman of obedience and my heart's greatest desire is to draw closer to you. Help me to never sacrifice my time with you. I pray that I allow you into the deepest and darkest parts of my heart and transparency will always flow. I pray against any shame or guilt from sin or embarrassment that would let me stray from your presence and derail me from coming to you. Prepare my heart for experiencing life by mending any brokenness or pain from my past. Help me seek you always and maintain the commitment to reading Your word and praying to experience intimacy with you God, like never before. I pray love rejuvenates my soul and reminds me just how much I love you.

In Jesus name I pray, Amen

CHAPTER 07

Loving Yourself

We love because he first loved us. (1 John 4:19)

In the midst of the world we are in, we have had the chance to have a lot of time to ourselves. A lot of time to sit and focus and sometimes negative thoughts can seep into our consciousness if we are not careful. To make manifest the glory of God that is within us we must stay connected to God and allow the very special light to shine through. You are special to God and adored by God, that's why honoring your temple and loving yourself is critical to developing your Christian walk.

I remember walking to my car one day after work. A lie had been told on me at work. I was confused, angry, and disappointed at myself for being dragged into the drama. I thought in my head, *God, I don't know why you put up with me.* At that moment, I felt the gentlest whisper in my spirit say, *I don't "put up" with you. I adore you.* Tears are welling up in my eyes even now as I remember that moment. God doesn't put up with you either. He adores you.

So often we project onto God how we feel about ourselves- full of disappointment, failure, and doubt. Oftentimes we also can project from a place of woundedness from our past—how our mom or dad talked to us when we were little, or how a hateful boyfriend or girlfriend treated us in high school. We expect that God feels the same way about us.

We have to realize that your biggest competitor is in the mirror. You are the first person to hear your thoughts. Words cut like knives. You don't have to believe what everyone tells you about yourself, especially if it does not agree with your spirit. If you have people around you who don't speak to your inner greatness, then you are going to live with their bitterness. Don't let them rob you of your inner-strength and light. Don't allow Satan to rent-free space in your head or heart. Give him an immediate eviction notice. LOVE COMES FROM GOD. Hating yourself is not of God but Loving yourself is of God. When we love ourselves, it is contagious. It then can spread to knowing how to love and honor others better and ultimately glorify God.

Ask yourself: What goals will help me Love myself and honor my body/vessel God more?

_____

_____

_____

_____

_____

_____

_____

_____

_____

_____

_____

_____

_____

_____

God Goals

- ☐ Cancel any negative self-talk

- ☐ Focus on your gifts

- ☐ Focus on your purpose

- ☐ Ask God to reveal your purpose and bring the right people in your life.

- ☐ Ask God to search your heart for any negative thought patterns and lies that you believed about yourself & subscribed to over the years and ask Him to remove them.

- ☐ Challenge your self-talk to always be positive

- ☐ Change your self- talk

- ☐ Make a list of positive things about yourself

- ☐ Make time and take time to do the things you love

- ☐ Make sure you have an adequate amount of solitude in your life.

Scripture Meditations

For no one ever hated His own flesh, but nourishes and cherishes it, just as Christ does the church (Ephesians 5:29)

I praise you because I am fearfully and wonderfully made; your works are wonderful; I know that full well. (Psalm 139:41)

Whoever gets sense loves His own soul; he who keeps understanding will discover good. (Proverbs 19:8)

To acquire wisdom is to love yourself; people who cherish understanding will prosper. (Proverbs 19:8)

You are altogether beautiful, my love; there is no flaw in you replied: "Love the Lord your God with all your heart and with all your soul and with all your mind.' This is the first and greatest commandment. And the second is like it: 'Love your neighbor as yourself.' (Song of Solomon 4:7)

You, dear children, are from God and have overcome them, because the one who is in you is greater than the one who is in the world. (1 John 4:4)

Don't you know that you yourselves are God's temple and that

God's Spirit dwells in your midst? If anyone destroys God's temple, God will destroy that person; for God's temple is sacred, and you together are that temple. (1 Corinthians 3:16-17)

Prayer

Heavenly Father, I ask that you help me to accept and love myself the way I am, without judgment. Help me to love myself as I am an extension and reflection of you Lord. Please allow the love that I have for myself to radiate so strong that it is contagious to others around me. I pray that I never would reject myself from happiness, freedom, and love. From this moment on allow every thought, emotion, or belief about myself to be rooted in love. Help me Lord to increase my self-love and decrease fear. When I reject myself, I reject you, Lord, help me to keep love in the driven seat of my mind, will, and emotions. Transform any anxiety, worry, or sadness into joy, peace, and happiness. Let the power of your Holy spirit break any lies that I was told as a child and as an adult. The lies that I believed and internalized, wash them away with your power and help me plant new seeds and produce new fruit. Help me take full responsibility to face any problem and resolve any situation as they arise. I pray that I will always count myself in rather than out, set myself up for love rather than down due to hate. Help me have the courage to facilitate and maintain positive and loving relationships with my family and friends that work together in perfect harmony for your good. Lord, help me enjoy the peace of my solitude, allow me to experience extreme peace in my presence. Cleanse me from any toxic emotions left from previous relationships and unhealed wounds from my past. Lord God create in me a new mindset that operates in gratitude, generosity, and love. Help me not to seek validation from the world, but only you Jesus, for I am fearfully and wonderfully made.

In Jesus name I pray, Amen

CHAPTER 08

Holy Hands

(TRY JESUS NOT ME)

*Examine me, O **LORD**, and prove me; Try my mind and my heart.*
(Psalm 26:2)

There has been plenty of times within the past year that I was angry, mad, upset, dismayed about different situations especially looking at the news. I felt vengeful, and with rage. At times we want to yell "Try me!" We cannot let our emotions cloud our better judgment or do something that will have permanent results based on a temporary feeling. The bible says be angry be sin not. (Ephesians 4:26) Whatever the origin of your anger, it can be very difficult to control and the enemy preys on our weak flesh and wounded ego to destroy us. Meditate within your heart on your bed and be still. (Psalm 4:4) How can you have good judgment when you act on emotion. You make irrational decisions that have no benefit to you in the end. Don't allow your emotions to overpower your intelligence Allow yourself to be still and let God work on your behalf.

What do you want your life to be filled with? Joy and satisfaction? Or anger and destruction? Be open to learning from your mistakes and develop your patterns to take you down a path towards greatness. It's critical to living the abundant life God has designed for you.

When anger threatens to overcome your compassion, remember God's devotion to you and His unending love. Despite our sins, God is gracious. The harmful rages of anger are reduced to pure ashes when we submit them to the Father. Our heavenly Father washes them away and leaves our heart and mind renewed and set free.

Ask yourself: What goals will help me channel my anger in peace?

_____

_____

_____

_____

_____

_____

_____

_____

_____

_____

_____

_____

_____

_____

_____

_____

_____

_____

_____

_____

_____

_____

_____

_____

_____

_____

_____

_____

_____

_____

_____

_____

_____

_____

_____

_____

God Goals

☐   Go to a quiet place

☐   Be still and listen to your heart

☐   Submit to the work of the Holy Spirit to keep yourself from sin.

☐   Allow God to calm your heart and speak to you in the quiteness.

☐   Know your triggers and be open to addressing those triggers and healing from them through prayer, counseling and/or therapy.

☐   Control the environment and company you keep. You cannot expect to not be triggered, angry and upset if you keep surrounding yourself with the very things that take you down the pathway to anger.

Scripture Meditations

Whoever has no rule over His own spirit is like a city broken down, without walls. (Proverbs 25:28)

A fool vent all His feelings, but a wise man holds them back. (Proverbs 29:11)

But the fruit of the spirit is love, joy, peace, long suffering, kindness, goodness, faithfulness, gentleman, self-control. Against such there is no law. (Galatians 5: 22-23)

Now the purpose of the commandment is love from pure heart, from a good conscience, and from sincere faith. (1 Timothy 1:5)

The LORD will fight for you, and you shall hold your peace. (Exodus 14:14)

And above all things have fervent love for one another, for "love will cover of multitude of sins." (1 Peter 4: 8)

Dear friends, let us love one another, for love comes from God. Everyone who loves has been born of God and knows God. [8] Whoever does not love does not know God, because God is love. (1 John 4:7-8)

Do not lay hands on anyone hastily. (1 Timothy 5:22)

My dear brothers and sisters, take note of this: Everyone should be quick to listen, slow to speak and slow to become angry. (James 1:19)

You, O Lord, are a God full of compassion, and gracious, longsuffering, and abundant in mercy and truth. (Psalm 86:15)

Prayer

Dear Heavenly Father, I confess that too often, I allow myself to be controlled by my desires and my impulses rather than by Your Spirit. Please forgive me and help me to draw me closer to You, walking in Your Spirit every moment of every day. Decrease me and increase you within me. I pray that my character is a direct reflection of you. Anoint my speech and every word that comes out of my mouth. I pray that I will have conviction in my heart to have control over my tongue and be quick to use my words to affirm others. The treasures in my heart produce good fruit that is evident to all. Surround me with the right people who will help lead and guide me. Keep me humble and always willing to learn. If there are any foolish tendencies within me, remove it Lord, and mold me into a mature man or woman of God. Your peace surpasses all my understanding. When anger rises within me, please calm my mind and soothe my heart with your gentle words. Fill my whole life with your perfect peace. May my personality be shaped by your peace rather than my frustration. With your Holy Spirit in my life, I can overcome anger. May I reflect your character, being slow to anger and rich in steadfast love. Look upon me and cause your face to shine upon me. Lord, bring peace to my mind and my heart as I feel angry at any situation, that I am in. May I take hold of your promise that you will never leave me nor forsake me. In whatever circumstances I face that produce anger in my heart, remind me that you have not left my side and you never will. When you are with me, I can trust you to fight my battles, I do not need to allow anger to take control. Give me your peace Father, may it rule over my life.

In Jesus Christ, that I pray. Amen

CHAPTER 09

Remain In Me

"Remain in me, as I also remain in you. No branch can bear fruit by itself; it must remain in the vine. Neither can you bear fruit unless you remain in me. ~ (John 15:4)

S taying anchored to God requires a daily decision to submit to our heavenly Father's will and direction for our lives. God will not push himself on you. He will not share His glory with another, and he will not try to compete with the world for your heart. But if you draw near to him, he will wrap you in the sweetness, love, and power of His presence. Welcome him into your life today and every day.

Sometimes we feel distant from God, the beautiful truth is that he has not gone anywhere. He remains in the same place that we meet him and is forever unwavering and unchanging. God never turns His back on His children and His heart is open and always to be with us. Awhile ago when I was going back and forth between the world and serving God, Sundays were the only day I read the bible, listen to praise in worship music, and prayed. Monday through Saturday was a free for all and I did what I wanted to do. I was what you would call a "Sunday morning Christian." I didn't chase God and I wasn't focused on remaining in His presence until something tragic happened and I felt like I needed him most. I would run to God when I was in trouble, like a small child. My faith was child-like and it had no anchor, consistency, or maturity. I was decorated with the word on Sunday's but I was not embodying living the word through my actions.

The true story is that I will always need to be in the presence of God. God wants to live through us and be the living word in our lives. Our behavior, actions, goals should reflect the glory of God and all that he has done and blessed us with in life. We cannot claim to know him and love him if we are not living by His word. Remain connected to the heavenly Father at all times and seek the kingdom first and all these things will be added to unto you! (Matthew 6:33)

Ask yourself: What goals will help remain connected to God every day?

_____

_____

_____

_____

_____

_____

_____

_____

_____

_____

_____

_____

_____

_____

God Goals

☐ Share what God has done for you. Let your testimony be able to bless someone else who may be going through a similar experience.

☐ Do something for someone else. Do it from the heart without expecting anything in return.

☐ Use the gifts that God has gave you. We all have something to give to the Kingdom of God. It may not look the same. If you were called to sing, write, minister, create, sew, usher, find out what that is and honor God with those gifts.

☐ Be grateful . Count everything joy and be grateful for His blessing everyday.

☐ Fast & Pray. Fasting can bring us ultimately clarity and allow us to have a breakthrough encounter with God like never before.

Scripture Meditations

And be found in him, not having a righteousness of my own tha comes from the law, but that which is through faith in[a] Christ— the righteousness that comes from God on the basis of faith. (Phillipians 3:9)

The eyes of the LORD are on the righteous, and His ears ar attentive to their cry; (Psalm 34:15)

filled with the fruit of righteousness that comes through Jesu Christ—to the glory and praise of God. (Philippians 1:11)

Finally, brothers and sisters, whatever is true, whatever is noble whatever is right, whatever is pure, whatever is lovely, whatever i admirable—if anything is excellent or praiseworthy—think abou such things. (Philippians 4:8)

But you, man of God, flee from all this, and pursue righteousness godliness, faith, love, endurance, and gentleness. (1 Timothy 6:11

Come close to God, and God will come close to you. Wash you hands, you sinners; purify your hearts, for your loyalty is divide between God and the world. (James 4:8)

When you follow the revelation of the word, heaven's bliss fills your soul. (Proverbs 29:18)

Prayer

Heavenly Father, I thank you for today, for you are all-powerful, all-knowing, and intentional! Continue to mold me like clay in the potter's hand. Help me be the person you created me to be. I know you have a divine purpose for my life. I pray that I can continue to mature into the man/woman of God that you have called me to be. Help me to think clearly, act respectfully, and love deeply. I pray that I will put away childish ways and embrace the responsibilities of a man/woman of God that you have assigned me to be. I pray that I still know how to embrace laughter and fun in life, but be serious about you Lord. Bring balance, understanding, patience, love, and kindness in my life and allow me to continue to operate in the fruits of the spirit. I pray that my current/future spouse will be anchored in you as well and we can blossom together in your name. Holy spirit anoint me and mature me as I stay connected, grow, develop, and be shaped by you Lord. Help me to operate in selflessness, humility, and gentleness as you mature my character, perspective and attitude. Transform my heart and prepare me for all that you have for me!

In Jesus name I pray, Amen

Prayer of Salvation

Heavenly father, I come to you from the depths of my heart realizing I have sinned. I repent of my sins and confess with my mouth that Jesus Christ is the son of God and died on the cross for me and my sins. I believed that you raised him from the dead. Lord Jesus come into my heart and live in me now. I receive by faith You as my personal Lord and Savior. I receive your Holy Spirit as my comforter to help me obey You, and do your will. Come into my life Jesus and it is in Jesus name that I believe and receive in the things prayed this day.

Amen

Acknowledgements

Thank you God for blessing me to see this journey complete. May this book go on to inspire greatness, impact lives, and empower youth, young adults, and anybody that needs God goals in their life. Lord, I understand I am the vessel and messenger of the great works that you are doing within me.

Thank you to Millennials on the Move! My brothers and sisters in Christ. Never in my wildest dreams that I think our connect grow would grow to what it is today. I thank you all for joining and showing up to contribute to a safe space where we can bask in God's presence weekly through fellowship, praise, and honor God on Friday nights. See you Friday!

Mrs. Cherie Banks, thank you for being an awesome mentor and friend. Thank you for always taking time out of your schedule to stop and see about me and make time to talk, chat, and pray!

To my beautiful family, friends, sister-friends, colleagues, supporters! I love you all so much for contributing your words of encouragement along this journey.

With much love and gratitude,

Shanté Berry

A note about the author

Shanté Berry is a writer, poet, mentor, social entrepreneur, public speaker and a catalyst for positive change. She is a product of the Saint Louis Public Schools system. She graduated from Gateway Institute of Technology High School and Xavier University of Louisiana. She has worked and written for Essence Magazine and developed her own editorial blogs. She is also a health care finance specialist working in the field of education. Driven by her obstacles and miracles in life, she transforms everything she has experienced into motivation for herself and others to succeed. She has a deep passion for health, literacy & continuing a legacy of excellence. She seeks to empower and enhance her community through literacy, mentoring, and motivation. She loves spending time with her family, laughing, writing, and traveling. She believes that literacy can change lives and if you open a book, your world will open as well. Ms. Berry currently resides in Texas.